The Dragonfly Story

Explaining the death of a loved one to children and families

Written by Kelly Owen   Illustrated by Helen Braid

THE DRAGONFLY STORY 978-1-9999965-0-5

First published in Great Britain by Ultimate Publications
This edition published 2018
Text copyright © Kelly Owen, 2018
Illustrations copyright © Helen Braid, 2018
The right of Kelly Owen and Helen Braid to be identified
as the author and illustrator of this work has been asserted
in accordance with the Copyright, Designs and Patents Act 1988.
All rights reserved. No part of this publication may be reproduced,
stored in a retrieval system, or transmitted in any form or by any means,
electronic, mechanical, photocopying, recording or otherwise,
without the prior permission of the publisher.

www.chasingdragonfliesblog.com

Ultimate Publications is a trading name of
Ultimate Proof Ltd. Reg no. 07720107

A CIP catalogue record for this book is available from the British Library.
Printed in the UK by Acorn Press Ltd, Swindon.

For Abigail Emily Owen, forever smiling,
and Baby Bella.

Also in loving memory of:

Allegra Whittome
Andrew Butland
Bear
Daniel George Wilford
Jackson John Yates
Jacob Ryder Wiggins
Lauren Kimberley Roberts
Martha Mary Stanley-Duke
Peter Baldwin
Phoebe Casson
Samuel Ian Gardner
Sophia Neasmith

whose parents and friends have helped contribute
towards the publication of this first edition.

Also loving thanks to family, friends and all those
who helped bring this book to print.

The Owen family were feeling sad.

There used to be five of them.
There was Mum, Dad and three children:
Abi, Jenny and Joe. But then Abi died.
Now there were only four of them.

Life felt very strange without their sister, and they were all very, very unhappy.

Jenny missed the bed-time chats she had with Abi the most.

Joe missed the funny games Abi would play with him.

They had lots of happy memories of their sister, but wondered where she had gone.

"Where is Abi now?" asked Joe.
"She's dead," Jenny replied in a quiet voice.

"But where is dead? Where has she gone?" he asked.
"I don't know," Jenny said. "Heaven, I suppose."

Mum and Dad overheard them talking.
"Come on, let's go to the park," Dad said.

They went to the big park which had a large boating lake. Mum and Dad always brought them here to play. They hadn't been to the park since Abi died. They hadn't felt like playing there without her.

But today was sunny and it felt nice to be outside again.

Mum and Dad unpacked the picnic while Jenny and Joe played with their dog, Darcy.

Darcy ran over to play by the lake, and Jenny spotted a pretty blue dragonfly darting from leaf to leaf.

"Look Mum, a dragonfly! It looks like it's dancing."

"Dragonflies are beautiful insects," said Mum. "It's quite special to see one up close. It reminds me of the dragonfly story. Would you like to hear it?" "Yes please," Jenny said and she sat down on the picnic rug. As they ate their sandwiches, Mum told them the story of the water nymphs and dragonflies.

Deep down, at the bottom of a lake just like this, lived small brown bugs called nymphs. They were quite happy, scuttling along the mud, in the dark, cool water.

Sometimes, one of the nymphs would want to cling to the stem of a nearby plant.

Ever so slowly, the nymph would climb the plant until it had gone up through the surface of the water, and the other nymphs wouldn't see it again.

One day, a nymph said to her friends, "Do you see that nymph over there? He's going up to the sky."

They watched as the nymph slowly climbed up a stem and disappeared above the water. They waited for a while, but he didn't come back.

"Where do you think he has gone?" she asked. "Didn't he want to stay here with us?" asked another nymph, sadly. "When will he come back?" wondered a third.

"I know!" said the first nymph. "When one of us goes up to the sky, we must come back down again and tell the others what is up there."

"Good idea," the other nymphs agreed.

Sometime after, that same nymph felt she wanted to climb up a plant. She took hold of the stem and slowly climbed up and up to the sky.

When she reached the surface of the water, the nymph burst through into the bright sunshine. She was tired now, so holding the top of the stem tightly, she closed her eyes and fell asleep in the warmth of the sun.

When the nymph opened her eyes,
she looked about in wonder.
Everything was so light and beautiful.

She looked down at her reflection in the water and saw her old bug body had completely changed. She had turned into a dragonfly! She now had an amazing long blue tail.

She gave a little wriggle and stretched. Four beautiful silver wings fluttered in the breeze. With a whoosh, she lifted up and flew high above the water.

The sparkling new dragonfly dipped and swooped around in the bright sunshine. She skimmed along the water's surface.

She felt so free!

After a while, she landed on a plant to rest and looked about. She was so happy and relaxed in this beautiful place.

She looked down at the water to admire her reflection and spotted the nymphs at the bottom of the lake far below.

"There's my family and friends, I said I would go back to tell them what it's like," she remembered.

She tried to dive down to see them, but her beautiful dragonfly body bounced off the surface of the water. Now the nymph had become a dragonfly, she couldn't go under the water again.

"Oh, I can't go back to see them," she said, sadly. "I'll just have to wait until it's their turn to become dragonflies and come up to see me. Then they will know where I went, and we can be together again."

So the dragonfly flew off to explore her new world in the sunshine and gentle breeze.

"Do you think Abi is like a dragonfly now?" asked Joe when the story was finished.

"We are all a bit like the little nymphs living under the water, on Earth," said Jenny. "And Abi has gone somewhere like the place above the water… like heaven."

"So, when we die, perhaps we change into something more beautiful too, like the nymphs into dragonflies," Joe said.

"That's a nice way to think of it," said Mum. "We all miss Abi very much; we didn't want her to leave us so soon. We believe she has gone to a place where she can be peaceful and happy, just like a beautiful dragonfly flying around a lake in the sunshine."

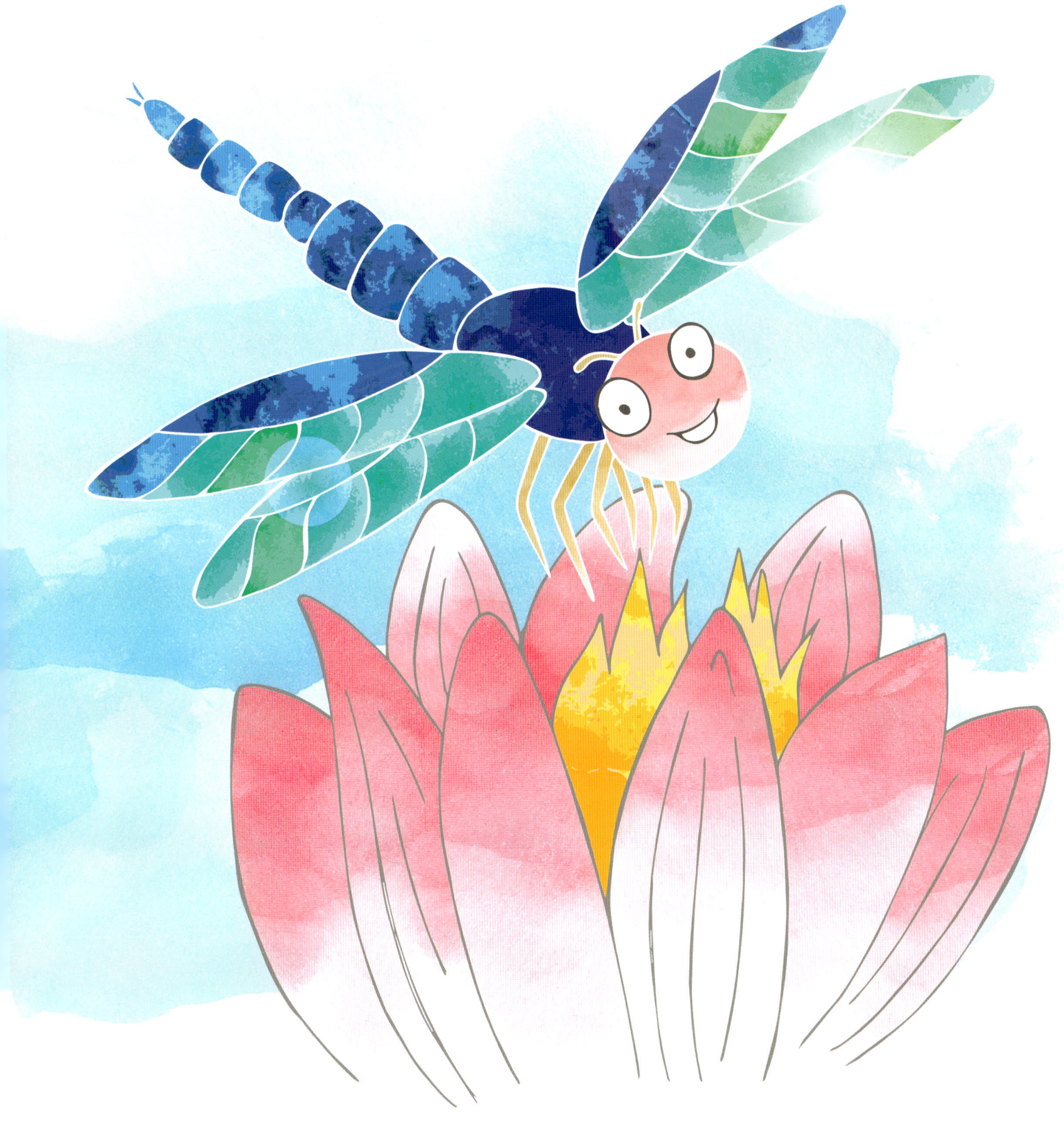

Mum, Dad, Jenny, Joe and Darcy spent a lovely afternoon playing by the boating lake.

Every now and then a dragonfly would dance around with them,
reminding them of their lively and happy sister.

About the author

Kelly Owen was inspired by the fable of the waterbugs and dragonflies following the death of her eldest daughter, Abi, in 2013. The simple concept led to the creation of her blog, Chasing Dragonflies, which recounts her journey through grief and adjustment to the loss of her child. She always believed the story could be colourfully presented and adapted to help children understand losing a close family member, with a focus on the hope of heaven and peace.
Kelly lives in Gloucestershire with her husband, Mark, and their four children: Jen, Joe and two rainbows, Jake and Naomi.
www.chasingdragonfliesblog.com

About the illustrator

Helen Braid lives on the beautiful Northumberland coast which is a constant source of inspiration for her illustrations. Helen first met Kelly when she was commissioned to produce the artwork for her blog. She works from her cottage studio surrounded by pens, watercolours, and cups of cappucinno.
www.ellieillustrates.co.uk